D1118750

Meow*

The Somewhat Comprehensive Book of Cat Names

Faye Passow

* Cats will ask for it by name.

First Edition
09 08 07 06 05   5 4 3 2 1

Text and illustrations © 2005 Faye Passow

Published by
Gibbs Smith, Publisher
P.O. Box 667
Layton, Utah 84041

Orders: 1.800.748.5439
www.gibbs-smith.com

Designed by Faye Passow
Printed and bound in the United States of America

Library of Congress Cataloging-in-Publication Data

Passow, Faye.
 Meow : the somewhat comprehensive book of cat names / by Faye Passow.—
1st ed.
    p. cm.
  ISBN 1-58685-737-1
 1. Cats—Names. I. Title.

SF422.4.P27 2005
929.9'7—dc22

2004023354

C is for

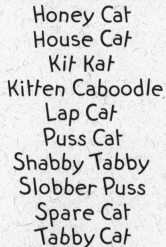

Alley Cat	Honey Cat
Average Cat	House Cat
Barn Cat	Kit Kat
Cat Ballou	Kitten Caboodle
Cat Boy	Lap Cat
Curious Cat	Puss Cat
Fat Cat	Shabby Tabby
Ginger Cat	Slobber Puss
Hell Cat	Spare Cat
Hep Cat	Tabby Cat

Feed me!
Pet me!
But don't try
to get me!

That's my name. Don't wear it out.

Abner	Gus	Abbey	Miranda
Ajax	Higgins	Ava	Mitzy
Awden	Hobson	Bess	Muffy
Beal	Iggy	Dolly	Nina
Bilco	Link	Edith	Nivah
Bob	Murphy	Elsa	Odessa
Calvin	Onslow	Gidget	Pearl
Cato	Otis	Jennifur	Sophie
Cosmo	Ozzie	Lola	Sylvia
Dave	Sammy	Lucinda	Tabatha
Dexter	Seymore	Lulabelle	Wanda
Elwood	Wendell	Marilla	Zelda

Sammy

Victorian

Aaron	Alva
Aloishious	Clarissa
Ambrose	Clementine
Archibald	Edwina
Bartholomew	Esmeralda
Bertram	Hortense
Clarence	Nellie
Horatio	Rowena
Leander	Selina
Obediah	Victoria
Zebulon	Vivian

Purebreds

Abernathy	Cordelia	Montague
Allegra	Eugenia	Narcissa
Aureole	Evangeline	Oberon
Battina	Fauntleroy	Ophelia
Belvedere	Felicity	Priscilla
Bentley	Gladstone	Rothschild
Broderick	Graves	Sebastian
Buckminster	Heathcliff	Valmont
Churchill	Minerva	Wellington

Cats in Hats

Familiarity
Breeds
Contempt!

Captain Flash	Miss Congeniality
Chairman Meow	Miss Jingles
Count Pounce	Miss Manners
Dr. Doeslittle	Miss Priss
General Muff	Mr. Bickles
Herr Ball	Mr. Bizzy
Judge Mental	Mr. So and So
Le Docteur	Mr. Underfoot
Madame Vanity	The Boss

Hats on Cats

French Chats

Anaïs, Adrien, Babette, Brigitte,
Camille, Céleste, Chantal, Claude,
Colette, Danièle, Dominique, François,
Gaston, Gisèlle, Genevieve, Gustave,
Henri, Hermione, Joséphine, Luc,
Mignon, Poirot, Réne, Sabine, Seurat,
Simone, Sophie, Yves, Yvette

EGYPTIAN
CATS

Amenhotep	Imhotep
Amenti	Isis
Amun-Ra	Nefertiti
Anubis	Nofret
Bastet	Osiris
Buto	Ra
Cleopatra	Ramses
Hammurabi	Tefnut
Horus	Thoth
Rahotep	Tutankhamen

Pwitty Whittle Kitty
❀ Names ❀

Babykins
Bitzie-pookums
Boodle-ookins
Bumblekins
Chubby Bumpkins
Chubby-wubby
Cutsy-wootsie
Fuzzy-muzzle
Pwitty Whittle Puddy Tat

Pookins
Poopsie
Puddin' Head
Punkin Pooh
Schnookums
Snickle Fritz
Snuffykins
Snuggle Pooh

OH MY! WHAT A
WONDERFUL CAT!

Bing-badda-bing

Bodeodoh

Bojangles

Bo Diddly

Ditty-what-ditty

Fiddle-dee-dee

Hey Diddle-diddle

Hullabalo

Do-what-kitty-kitty-do

Inka-dinka-do

Mewsette

Pitter Pat

Razzmatazz

Shabooboo

Shim-shim-shiree

Ting-a-ling

Zippity-do-dah

CATS WITH RECESSIVE GENES

Bimbo	Furrball	Pidge
Boodle	Grizzle	Shtinky
Bubba	Gummo	Simpkin
Deeber	Meems	Smitty
Doofus	Miscreant	Toofles
Filbert	Norton	Varminton
Frazzle	Piddle	Wumps

FERAL CATS

Bad Leroy
Demonette
Destructo
Dracula
Dragon Lady
Drama Queen
Hades
Hellweasel
Hobgoblin

Ignatz Badcatsky
Inate Savage
Inferno
Jeckles
Mr. McNasty
Nasty Piece
Nemesis
Pretty Boy Floyd
Satan's Sister
Skid Rogue
Voo Doo

EARTHLY CATS

Cyclone	Mirage
Doppler Radar	Misty Glen
Dusk	Nightshade
Dust Devil	Shadowfoot
Fireball	Smokey
Foggy Bottoms	Twilight
Frosty	Typhoon

Heavenly Katz

Asteroid	Moonbeam
Big Bang	Moondance
Black Hole	Nebulous
Blue Comet	Sky Rocket
Cassiopeia	Space Cadet
Dark Matter	Space Ranger
Galaxy	Stargazer
Mir	Zenith

COLORS

Azure	Merlot
Cappuccino	Mocha
Charcoal	Niello
Ebony	Periwinkle
Indigo	Raven
Ivory	Sage
Magenta	Scarlet
Mahogany	White Pearl

DARE I REPEAT MYSELF

Bon Bon   Mish Mish
Boom Boom   Picky Picky
Can-Can   Plink Plink
Choo Choo   Pom-Pom
Gin Gin   Tom Tom
Gris Gris   Tum Tum
Kitty Kitty   Yam Yam
Mini Mini   Zsa Zsa

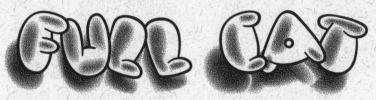

FULL CAT

Brown Sugar
Butterbean
Cheese Ball
Chiffon
Cinnamon
Creampuff
Crumpet
Doughnut
Fizzy

Fruitcake
Gazpacho
Lady Fingers
Licorice
Macaroni
Marmalade
Mayo
Meatball
Milktoast
Nutmeg
Parsley

Peaches
Popcorn
Puddin'
Raisin
Rumball
Saphron
Snickerdoodle
Spumoni
Sugarpuss
Tabasco
Toffee

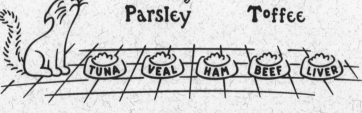

TUNA   VEAL   HAM   BEEF   LIVER

FAT CAT

Baby Giant
Benny the Ball
Big Foot
Big Kahuna
Big Minnie
Blob Cat
Bulky Bob
Chubbette
Chunky
Circular Sam

Colossus
Fatty Lumpkin
Gargantua
Goliath
Hulk
Lardo
Mr. Big Stuff
Orbicular Olaf
Plush Peg
Tubby

Brobdingnagian

FLOWER POWER

BLOSSOM	JASMINE
BLUEBELL	JOHNNY JUMP-UP
BUTTERCUP	JONQUIL
CAT-O'-NINE TAILS	LIRIOPE
COLUMBINE	MAGNOLIA
DANDELION	PETAL
DATURA	PRIMROSE
GARDENIA	SHRINKING VIOLET
JACK-IN-THE-PULPIT	TIGER LILY

ALL FOR FUN!

CHUBALUB
CRUMBLEBUM
FLEABITUS
FLIBBERTIGIBBET
GEE WILLIKERS
KERFUFFLE
KITTY WAMPUS
PEEKABOO

PIP-SQUEAK
POUNCESQUICK
PUZZLEPUSS
RAGAMUFFIN
RAPSCALLION
SCALAWAG
SNAGGLEPUSS
SNICKLEFRITZ
SNUFFLUFFLAFAGUS
STINKERBELL

Borrowed

Fingers

Bangles   Firecracker   Mittens

Bibs   Glitter   Mohair

Blaze   Hairball   Ping-Pong

Bobbin   Polka Dot

Boots   Puffball

Bristles   Satin

Cameo   Slippers

Cashmere   Sneakers

China   Static Cling

Confetti   Tatters

Crystal   Thumbs

Cuffs   Tiddlywinks

Emerald   Tomahawk

Feathers   Velvet

Puss 'n Slippers

Copy Cat!

Alien	Critter	Ocelot
Android	Cyclops	Piglet
Bat Face	Dancer	Pinhead
Bobcat	Fairy	Possum
Bozo	Geisha	Puma
Cadaver	Gringo	Raven
Chimera	Leopard	Saint
Clown	Lion	Scrooge
Cougar		Sloth

NARCOLEPTICAT

Couchant Cosmo   Dormant Dagmar
El Placid   Flaccid Fenks
Idle Lupita   Inert Igor
Latitudinal Lonigan
Loitering Lolita   Lolling Lloyd
Melancholy Mogenson
Morose Mumphreys
Motionless Mertense
Procumbent Percival
Quiescent Quimby
Slothful Siegfried
Slumberous Sidlow
Torporous Throckmorton
Vegetative Viv

ACTION FIGURES

Antic	Dizzy	Rumpus
Babbler	Fidgets	Slinky
Blur	High Jump	Slurpy
Bouncer	Nitro	Smudge
Carom	Oratorio	Sneaky
Chaser	Peekers	Squishy
Chuckles	Ricochet	Tippy
Contorta	Riddles	Tiptoes
Dash		Zip

Handles

Ace of Spays   Bigwig Tig
Claw-Foot Tubby
Clive the Carpet King
Heat-Seeking Bissel
Jumping Jehoshaphat
Lewis the Lactose Tolerant
Knight Arrogant   Merry-Go-Rhonda
Osbert the Friendly Critic
Polly Dactyl-Doodle-All-A-Day
Sam Spayed   Tit-For-Tat Cat
Sheba the Sofa-Opera Queen
Walk-About Wendel

ONE+ONE

Busy Boy & Dream Girl
Jaqueline & Heidi
Needles & Pinhead
Meathead & Carrot Top
Family Circle & Bermuda Triangle

Search & Destroy   Rough & Tumbles
Bubble & Squeak   Nancy & Sluggo
Hodge & Podge   Death & Taxes
Early & Curly   Herb & Spices
Dodge & Dart   Youth & Asia
Furm & Phat   Ants & Pants
Rose & Bud   Ex & Why

"Catango"

Sesquipedalian Delights

Acroy the Ambuscade
Altisonant Arbuckle
Appressive Amelia
Bumptious Bramley
Burton the Bushwacker
Cirumvolant Sinclair
Contumecious Curtis
Coshered Carol
Delitescent Dupre
Divagating Darnell
Heliotropic Hayslet
Jickles the Jobbernowl
Lackadaisical Lambert
Maladroit McGillicuty
Marshall the Monocraticat

Peregrine the Panjandrum
Plangorous Prunella
Pudlenka the Popinjay
Querimonious Morticia
Supercilious Schminkus
Tristan the Tatterdemalion

Coshered
Carol

Straight from the
Phone Book

ALLZDAY, Slumber
BENTON, Tail
CARNIVORA, Shirley
CAT, Al E.
CAT, Leah Z.
COUCH, Rex Z.
GORA, Ann
HAPPY, S. Lap
KEETEE, B. Z.
KISMET, Cat O.
LAPINSKY, Idle

LUSTER, B.
MANGE, Tom E.
MOUSEHATTAN, Chase
SHREDDER, Sophia
TAILER, Liza B.
TAILMENT, Curl
TAUNT, Deb U.
TIN-TREAT, Snubs
TONIC, Cat O.
WAUL, Cat R.

"Rex Z. COUCH"

"Sophia SHREDDER"

Shapely
Cats

Blob	Munchkin
Compressa	Nubbins
Critical Mass	Pipit
Dainty Mae	Pixie
Dinky	Sawed-off Sam
Fubsy	Short Change
Gordita	Testy Tidbit
Itty Bit	Thumbelina
Kewpie	Tinkerbell
Lilliput	Tiny Tabby

Strange (but true)

Bippity
Boppo
Choick
Ewart
Gavorta
Gazork
Lutz
Narcle

Naxle
Nebble
Rimpo
Snurg
Thilco
Thoby
Toofles
Wumps